CONTENTS

© Richardson George 2003

Telephone: 1-868-683-9048
E-Mail: rgeorge4000@gmail.com

THAT WILL NEVER HAPPEN TO ME

Biblical Principles on Abstinence, Overcoming Sexual Temptations and Avoiding the Unequal Yoke

Richardson George

WHY THIS IS IMPORTANT TO YOU

Several years ago, I had an eye-opening experience as I conversed with a young lady in her late teens. At the end of the conversation, I realized that she was married at age 17 and separated from her husband one month after their marriage. I cannot help but wonder what could have gone wrong. As a young person, was she aware of the nature of relationships? Did she follow basic principles that produce a happy and lasting relationship? Was she unaware of those principles or did she ignore them and deliberately broke them? Was she ready for marriage? Whatever the case may be, the end result was tragic – another broken precious young life, but you may say that will never happen to me.

The reality is that youths are at a critical stage in their lives where they think about the opposite sex and how they should relate to each other. They are constantly bombarded by thoughts of relationships and sex. They see it on TV, read it in books, hear it in today's music and hear it from their friends who "brag" about their experiences. Consequently, youths in general and Christian youths, in particular, sometime feel confused or pressured to try what their friends describe so glamorously. They sometimes wonder if something is wrong with them because "everybody" seems to be doing it. But how should they respond to these daily pressures? What does the Bible teach about relationships and sex? **Whenever the word relationship is used here it means at least having a boyfriend or girlfriend and includes more serious relationships.**

As the pastor and interim youth leader, I decided not to leave it to chance, but under the direction of the Holy Spirit, to teach our youths on this important issue. It is already in their minds, and I wanted to fulfill my responsibility of teaching them the biblical principles concerning relationships and sex at a level that is appropriate to them.

3

The information below is based on a series of discussions conducted by Pastor Richardson George with the youths of the Gasparillo Open Bible Church. However, you will find the information in this booklet very useful and practical regardless of your background. The topic *"That Will Never Happen To Me"* was introduced in October of 2001 and ended in February 2002. Much of what was said is included here (not necessarily in the same order) with some additional thoughts to complement and fine-tune those discussions. This booklet actually weaves together a report of the discussions and teachings on this vital topic.

The opening question was, "Would you like to get married one day?" There were different responses from those present. Some said "Yes", some "No" or "NOT ME" and others did not know. With that question, our attention was focused on relationships between the opposite sexes.

Getting married might be one of your goals in life, but before that, there are some important things that you need to consider and be aware of. The other sessions focused on youth and relationships until the climax some months later.

In keeping with the title, *"That Will Never Happen To Me,"* I placed emphasis on the dangers and pitfalls regarding relationships. I also gave attention to what the Bible teaches on relationships in light of real-life situations and temptations. The Bible is God's guidebook for life, and it has enough information to guide us in the choice of a boyfriend, girlfriend or spouse and how to develop a relationship that would bring respect to us and glory to God.

Question: Why do people think about girlfriend, boyfriend or sex at a certain age or stage in their lives?

Admittedly, some youths do not think about those things. Some postpone the issue until later in life. However, there are others who think about them and express their thoughts, while there are others who think about them but are afraid to

say so. The fact is that those thoughts will come to everyone at some stage in life, earlier for some and later for others. Nevertheless, such thoughts are generally triggered by:
1. **Biological changes**
2. **External influences**

1. Biological changes

The human body undergoes definite changes while growing up. This growing-up process is controlled by a tiny organ in the brain called the pituitary gland. This gland tells the rest of your glands what to do. New chemicals/hormones are produced leading to physical and psychological changes in preparation for adult life. These new chemicals will stir you to develop an appetite and interest in people of the opposite sex. You begin to take notice of or try to attract the opposite sex. You begin to think about "how yuh looking."

This is a natural part of your development as a whole person, but you still have the responsibility to "control your hormones."

2. External influences

These are the things that surround you every day. Most of these influences come through what you see, hear or read, and much of it is filled with sex. They scream at you saying "Just do it," "Do it right now" or "Everybody's doing it." That's a lie. Everybody isn't doing it.

Chapter 1

FALLING IN LOVE

Falling is often the result of a slip or an accident. So don't fall when your heart is filled with love. Rather, watch your step and tread cautiously.

What does it mean to be in love? What is love? I asked the question: If you love someone and your parents do not agree with the relationship, what would you do? Some said they would try to reason with their parents and explain why they like the person. They would also listen to what their parents have to say. Obedience to your parents while you are under their care is very important. One person said, "elope" jokingly, but some people were not sure what elope meant. It means to run away with someone to live with him/her or to get married. At this point, I reminded the youths present of "Romeo and Juliet," two youths who liked each other badly and killed themselves because their parents disagreed with the relationship. I asked what they thought about that action? Someone said, "That is foolish," and all the other youths agreed. All level headed people know that it is foolish to kill oneself. It is generally felt that people who think about suicide are really not thinking straight.

You should not kill yourself for anybody or because of anybody. **Killing yourself is always foolish and useless.** The person who kills himself/herself dies, and the person he/she tries to hurt continues to live. It is really a waste to commit suicide. You lose now, and you lose in eternity. But sometimes under the pressure, the devil gets you to say "I don't care" or "I am fed up with..." – famous words of suicidal people. "Romeo and Juliet" thought that killing themselves together was love, but they were dead wrong.

If you have said to yourself "I will kill myself" at least once, then Satan has already placed a poison dart in your mind. If you don't get rid of it now, that same thought lodged in your mind might end up killing you, and you would have no one to blame but yourself. You have to get rid of that thought today by saying, "I will never kill myself" until you mean it. Then stop thinking or saying anything about killing yourself. How do you know that the thought is gone? When you never think or say, "I will kill myself." Every time the thought comes to your mind say, "I reject that thought in Jesus' name." Speak it out loud. If thoughts of killing yourself continue, I urge you to talk to an adult who can help you immediately. Don't think about killing yourself; think about living for Jesus and fulfilling your purpose for being born.

Is there a difference between love and infatuation? Young people sometimes get mixed up between love and infatuation and learn the difference the hard way. Infatuation is to inspire with foolish or shallow affection; an attraction that is really immature and will pass quickly. You might be infatuated with someone who is just "carrying you for a ride." 'For a ride,' some young ladies literally have 'gas brains' and some males with cars take advantage of that. Sometimes people carry you for a ride then dump you like garbage. That is what infatuation can lead to.

However, love is active, and it is seen by the good things you do for someone or the way you treat that person with respect and dignity. Love is not just a feeling but is responsible action. A person who is in love seeks the other person's best interest and is not in the relationship only for what he/she can get from the next person but more for what he/she can give to the other person. A person in love is willing to make sacrifices for the next person. When the time is right, build your relationship on the foundation of true love not puppy love. **I Corinthians 13:4-8a** gives the following

7

qualities of true love, *"Love is patient, love is kind. It does not envy, it does not boast, it is not proud. It is not rude, it is not self-seeking, it is not easily angered, it keeps no record of wrongs. Love does not delight in evil but rejoices with the truth. It always protects, always trusts, always hopes, always perseveres. Love never fails…"*

Examples From The Bible

1. <u>Amnon and Tamar</u> **(II Samuel 13:1-15)**
    This is an example of false love. Amnon was in love with his sister and obsessed with her. He spent time planning, then with a premeditated intent he got her alone and raped her. After raping her, he hated her with a greater hatred than the 'so called' love he had for her before. Was that love? Not at all, that was not love. That was lust out of control. Don't mistake your mere physical attraction to someone for love. That 'love' is only 'skin' deep. Sure, physical attraction plays a part in choosing a life partner, but real love is much more than that.
2. <u>Jacob and Rachel</u> **(Genesis 29)**
    This is an example of true love. Jacob was attracted to Rachel when he saw her, but his love for her was seen by the sacrifices he made for her over the years ahead. He worked for seven years to get her hand in marriage only to be deceived at the end. He had to labour for seven more years to get Rachel, and he did it joyfully because of the deep love he had for her. After those extra years, he married Rachel and took great care of her. That is real love.

Being in love with a certain person could wrong or dangerous for various reasons, for example:

1. <u>Who it is</u> –
(a). An unsaved person, that is, someone who has never

given his/her life to Jesus and living for Him. It is always wrong for a Christian to enter into a relationship with an unsaved person. A Christian should not have a boyfriend or girlfriend who is unsaved. This blunt statement summarizes a point that was made in every session. A detailed study will be given below.

(b). If the person is already married.

(c). If the person is of the same sex – men marrying men.

(d). If the person is in the relationship for selfish reasons etc.

2. Age – If there is a big age difference between you and the person you are in love with, that could be a sign of trouble ahead. Age often represents psychological development. A big age difference could mean a major difference in the way of thinking and responding to life's situations. You may be operating on two different frequencies or levels.

3. Loss of focus – If you are in love with a person and you are losing focus of important things, that relationship is doing more harm than good to you. If your spiritual life suffers, your school performance drops (It is recommended that while you are in school, you should concentrate on your school work and not on any boy or girl) or your work suffers, then you should think twice about continuing that relationship. A relationship should add to your life, not take away.

4. Unemployment – How would you respond to a young man who is "really on" but isn't working anywhere? Beware ladies. You should avoid getting into a relationship with someone who is unemployed. Why? You can't eat words, "lyrics," good looks or even love at breakfast time. Make sure the man is working first before you even think about having a serious relationship with him. You may just be friends, then suddenly you realize he is really nice and you start "going steady." Watch out. Some men move really quickly to propose or do other things. What would you do if he asks you to marry him and he is not employed? If you marry an unemployed man is you to "ketch," and you will

have no one to blame but yourself when you start to see "hell."

Young men if you are unemployed, leave the young ladies alone. Go and look for a job first then look for a woman. You shouldn't take responsibilities you cannot fulfill. God gave Adam a job first before He gave him a wife.

5. <u>Incompatibility</u> – This is a big word that simply means disagreement. If you love someone, you must at least have some things in common and some things that both of you like. I don't mean pretending to like something when the only thing you really like is the person's face or body. All you know is that the person "looking real good." Look at the following example of incompatibility. You may like to stay at home and the person you are interested in likes to do things away from home. You may end up spending very little time with each other, and what then? A simple thing like that could create serious problems.

You must have things in common while appreciating the differences between both of you. If you are always disagreeing and fighting now, that is a bad sign for the future. Don't pretend. Be real, and let your life say, "What you see is what you get" and hope the other person's life is saying the same thing, and don't be afraid to call it "quits" if things are not working out.

Be careful with whom you "fall in love." Keep your head on at all times, and don't be carried away by emotions. It is well known that when emotions are turned on, the brain is turned off. For some people, it takes one touch or one 'sweet talk' and they go "all the way." Make the right decisions now and you will be glad for the rest of your life.

Chapter 2

ACCEPTANCE

Friendship is another aspect of relationship that is very important to everyone. However, friendship often brings pressure to be like your friends and to do what they are doing. This is called peer pressure. Peer pressure is a real powerful force that youths and even adults face in life. The desire to be riding with the crew and gain the approval of friends is very strong. People want to be accepted.

This matter of acceptance especially by peers is a serious youth relationship issue, and some youths will do almost anything to gain it. In other words, they are willing to pay a price to get it, and sometimes that price is as high as their virginity (sexual purity), self-respect, individuality, spiritual life, relationship with people who love and care for them, sanity, education or eternal destiny – all just to be "in." How tragic!

Young people want to belong, and the first person or group to show acceptance and receive them with open arms wins their vote of confidence. It is sometimes difficult for youths to establish their own identity or to find themselves. They look for role models, friendships and relationships, and many times they find it in the wrong people. Often, they are people who are in the limelight, people who are popular in the eyes of the public or their peers. Youths who look up to them often don't know anything about their private struggles and feelings of emptiness. Often, your friends know something is missing in their lives, but they will never tell you that because they have an image to maintain. As long as they can fool you, they can 'rule' you.

You end up believing a lie and living a make belief life yourself. You end up following fakes. They put on a show, and you believe it is the real thing. They only put you on "scenes." You got "set up" and you didn't even realize it.

You think you have it made. Maybe too late you might realize that you were only used and abused and then refused. They throw you away like garbage. Like the news that reported two young men who were friends running from a crime scene. One was wounded, but the other "friend" left him on the ground to fend for himself. Each man to himself. Then is you to "ketch." Maybe some youths are like the young man who left home telling his mother, "Meh friends go handle meh." A few weeks later he was found murdered, execution style with his hands tied behind his back next to the dead body of one of his friends "who go handle him." Yuh think it easy. The saying is true that says "Your friends will carry you, but they don't bring you back." Too often the police bring them back to the jail or the ambulance to the hospital or the mortuary (a place to keep dead bodies). How sad. That has happened many times before, but it doesn't have to happen to YOU.

You "lime" together, go parties, maybe drink, smoke and do drugs, womanize or "manize," commit petty crimes or big crimes and much more, and you say that is excitement. That is the life. You are so wrong. You alone know that when you are by yourself, your life is empty and meaningless. Murder, robbery, sex and other pleasures do not fill the emptiness. Something is still missing. Your life is like a hollow shell. It is like a merry-go-round, moving but not going anywhere.

Sometimes young people take years to realize "this doh make sense." Some people never "wise up" and come to that realization. However, some people are honest enough to admit that there must be more to life. When they look at the emptiness and lack of purpose and direction in their lives, they can't help but think that there must be a better life.

It is said that "any dead fish can flow downstream with the current, but it takes a live fish with a strong backbone to swim against the current" like the salmon fish. In other words, any weak person can follow the crowd, but it takes a really strong person to stand for something good even against the crowd and their so-called friends.

That's why the Bible warns, *"wide is the gate and broad is the road that leads to destruction, and many enter through it. But small is the gate and narrow the road that leads to life, and only a few find it"* **(Matthew 7:23, 24, NIV).** Are you one of the many people on the road to destruction **(Revelation 20:15)** or one of the few people on the road to eternal life **(Revelation 21:1-4)**? Would you like to get off the road to destruction and get onto the road that leads to eternal life? Please read on to find out exactly how. I encourage you to get onto the road to eternal life, and if you are already on that road, remain on it because you would never regret it.

Chapter 3

BEING UNEQUALLY YOKED

"What if you as a Christian like someone who is very handsome/beautiful, intelligent and has all the good qualities and everything you would like in a boyfriend/girlfriend or husband/wife except for one thing; he/she is not a Christian. The person is not saved. What would you do?" Someone said, "The person could get saved." The majority said words to the effect that you should not get involved with the person.

Anyhow, after some discussion, there was general agreement that one should not get into a relationship with such a person – not even as a boyfriend or girlfriend. Let him/her get saved first. The first question you should ask should be, "Are you a Christian?" If the answer is "No," then you should keep off. It's that simple. Sometimes we complicate matters then wonder how we got in this mess. Always remember that having good qualities is no substitute for being saved even though some unsaved people may have better qualities than some Christians.

This matter of being unequally yoked is of great importance and should be given priority attention. I have seen many young people get into relationships with unsaved people and immediately began to go downhill in their spiritual life and even backslide. Some even got married, and they are "bawling" today with regret. You may say, "That will never happen to me," but you are so wrong. Still some people prefer to burn to learn.

There may be exceptions, but you should not live your life by exceptions. That is a recipe for disaster. It is better to live by the rules than by the exceptions. The Bible is clear and uncompromising in its guidelines for relationships. If you live by what the Bible says, you will be safe, and you would not have a thing to worry about or any regrets.

Question: What does the Bible actually say about getting into a relationship with an unsaved person?

II Corinthians 6:14 says, "Be not unequally yoked together with unbelievers: *for what fellowship has righteousness with unrighteousness? And what communion has light with darkness?"* That is a clear command not to get into any intimate relationship (of the mind, emotions or body) with an unsaved person. **Amos 3:3** asks, "Can two walk together unless they agree?" Implying that real harmony only comes from agreement.

II Corinthians 6:17 says, *"Wherefore come out from among them, and be ye separate, says the Lord."* To be separate means to draw a boundary line and stay on your side which should be God's side. Set a boundary for yourself that you will not cross. If you don't set clear boundaries for yourself, others will set them for you. That is disastrous, and you will suffer badly. If you have no boundaries, you will enter the danger zone and you will not even know it until you get burnt. You may say, "That will never happen to me," but I have heard better than you talk.

The Bible warns clearly about having a relationship with an unsaved person. You should stay away from that danger zone and then you will not get into trouble. This is not just talk. Look at the example of a lady who was saved for 35 years who said (on radio), "All of a sudden, I got married to a (a person of another religion who was not a Christian) person." Then things started to go bad. Of course. She stopped serving Jesus and her joy was gone. Naturally!

We know that people don't generally get married 'all of a sudden' just like that. She must have had a relationship with the unsaved man before marrying him. Whether other Christians knew and counselled her on the dangers of such a relationship, we don't know. Nevertheless, things started to change only when she confessed her sin and surrendered her life back to Jesus.

It is worth mentioning here that usually when someone has a relationship with an unsaved person he/she doesn't tell anyone about it, and the pastor is usually the last person to find out, if at all. The reason they don't tell anyone is because they know that somehow something is wrong with such a relationship and not too many people should know about it.

Testimony: Look now at the example of a young lady who visited the church. She asked if she could share her experience with our youths when she heard the announcement of what we were discussing in the youth group. The date was set, and she came and shared her testimony for about 30 minutes about being unequally yoked.

She was saved and involved in her local church, but she became interested in a young man that she described as "a cute darkie" that she wanted to know better. He was handsome, had good qualities and attended church occasionally (sometimes young men attend church when they want to get a girl in church), and she started a relationship with him. She assumed he was a Christian because he went to church occasionally, but she never asked the question seriously. They started going steady until they got married. He was on his best behaviour before marriage, and as soon as they got married 'all hell broke loose.' The man changed like a chameleon. The details are heart breaking to know the pain that young woman went through at the hands of the man with all the "good qualities." A few years later they were separated, and she was on the run for her life. So much for the "cute darkie" then! It was a well-disguised trap of the devil and she fell right into it. Watch out for that trap of the devil because you may be the next victim if you are not careful. Please be careful with your life. Make the right choices.

She shared her testimony with our youths hoping that no one would make the same mistake she made by getting involved with an unsaved person. May the Lord help the Christian youths of our nation and every person who reads this book not to make the same mistake. The safest thing would be to not have an unsaved boyfriend or girlfriend not even for a moment. That is the truth. Thank God for her willingness to share that testimony with us, and may the Lord use her to reach other youths who are tempted to fall into the same trap.

In **Deuteronomy 7:3, 4,** God gave a very stern warning to the children of Israel that they should not marry people who don't worship Him. God pronounced judgment in verse 4 when He said, *"the anger of the Lord will be kindled against you, and destroy you suddenly."* That is a serious judgment because it is a serious sin against God to marry an unsaved person. At that time God hated relationships between people who worshipped Him and those who didn't know Him, and He hates it just the same today.

In fact, God displayed His unrestrained anger against the unequal yoke in the book of Numbers. God had specifically instructed the Israelites not to marry people who did not share their beliefs. In **Numbers chapter 25**, the Israelite men were enticed by the gorgeous Moabite women and began to indulge in unlawful sexual activities with them. The Israelite men were swept off their feet by those seductive beautiful Moabite women. What was the result? The men were trapped and ended up worshipping the Moabite gods.

Then the anger of the Lord was kindled against Israel. It all started with their attraction to 'unsaved' women which led to involvement with them and ended in their deaths. By this time, people were weeping as they saw family members die. Suddenly one shameless man came 'sporting' his 'unsaved' woman before the people and in front of Moses. When Phinehas (the high priest's son) saw that, he took up a javelin and went into the man's tent and thrust the javelin through

17

both of them. Immediately, the judgment of God stopped when Phinehas took drastic action. That example shows clearly how much God hates the unequal yoke. To God, it is a very serious offence to get into a relationship with an unsaved person. God strongly condemns such relationships.

Nehemiah 13:23-27 also refers to God's condemnation of marriage with 'unsaved' women. Solomon's biggest downfall was his love for strange women and also 'too many women' **(II Kings 11:1-9).** The Bible gives clear warnings against getting involved in a relationship with an unsaved person. It is against God's will to do so and consequently it is a sin that will be judged.

Concerning ministry, what would you think if <u>all</u> the unmarried leaders and people in ministry at your church had relationships with unsaved people?

Since the teaching of the Bible is so clear to us, one of the implications is that any single saved person who enters a relationship with an unsaved person is blatantly disobeying God's Word and should not be functioning in any leadership position in church as long as such a relationship continues. This may sound harsh, but it is the biblical standard, and we should be willing to live by it. Would you like to make a commitment to live by this biblical standard of not having a relationship with an unsaved person and receive God's blessing? I urge you to do so.

Psalms 84:11 says, *"No good thing will he/[God] withhold from them that walk uprightly."* Walk uprightly and this promise is yours. God will send the right saved person for you at the right time.

Chapter 4

SEX AND ITS INFLUENCES

As a young person, what would you do if a young lady/man comes up to you and says, "I know a good secret place where we can go right now. We will be alone, and we can have some fun. Nobody will know that we are there." This is a real situation, and it is at this point some young men and young women fail to control their hormones and lose their virginity or even worse. They go and do their 'thing' thinking it is a big secret and they are fooling everybody – friends don't know, parents don't know, siblings don't know, nobody knows. Yeah right! Who yuh think yuh fooling? If you are doing that you will realize soon enough that you are only fooling yourself.

On the matter of human sexuality, someone said, "We have needs," yet "There is a difference between a need and an urge. We may die if our needs are not met, but we will not die if our urges and drives are not met. Food is a basic human need. Sex does not fall in the category of human need." If you don't eat, you will die. If you do not have sex, you will not die.

It was mentioned that we are bombarded by sex. Those present mentioned some things that they were aware of and even seen. One person said that her classroom is the "making out" classroom in her school. It was also mentioned that one high school student was sexually intimate with a married man and was 'fighting for him.' Many of those present were aware of a young South taxi driver who was involved in a crime and was chased and shot dead by the police. At the funeral, a few young girls, including students, were crying for him. Each one of them must have thought that she was the only woman in his life. They were all so wrong. He fooled all of them and used all of them, and they didn't know it. Deceivers are out there, so beware! Don't be a young man who fools ladies thinking that is being 'macho.' It will eventually catch up with you.

Testimony: A young lady present mentioned the sad experience of one of her friends. She related that her friend's parents always counselled and warned her about "that boy," but she was "harden" and never listened. She continued steady with the young man until, you know what happened. Yes! She got pregnant. Now, she has two children. The children's 'father' is not around, and she is seeing 'hell' now, having to 'mind' two children on her own. She is holding her head and bawling now. Whose fault is that? Someone might say, "It is her fault, and she look for that." She made one serious mistake that she has to live with for the rest of her life. It didn't have to be so, but she chose that for herself. The man is also guilty of displaying criminal behaviour by abandoning the two children – the typical absentee father. None of that has to happen to you.

Whether male or female, I hope you are one of the youths who listen to the caring adults in your life. They have your best interest in mind, and many times they see and know things that you cannot see and don't know. Many youths and singles have taken the good advice of mature, caring adults and are happy today for listening to them. They have grown up to be respectable and responsible citizens of society. So can you. Please listen to those who have travelled that road before you. Listen, learn and think before you act.

Sexual Influences

Let us now identify some of the sexual influences that surround us. What are those things that pressure people to seriously consider having sex now or sometime soon or any time before marriage? Many voices are screaming, "You need to have sex now because everybody is doing it." It is very reassuring and refreshing to know that everybody isn't doing it. In the midst of declining moral and spiritual values, many single people have chosen to remain pure. I encourage you also to remain pure and retain your virginity until marriage and you will be so glad you did and also reap the benefits of purity. Later in this book some practical and biblical reasons why you should abstain from (avoid) sex until you are married will be given. The following are some common sexual influences.

1. Television

On TV, especially shows with young people, you see them kissing in the school's corridor – not on the cheek but mouth to mouth "resuscitation." You also see a woman advertising a brand of soap. At the end of the advertisement, she sits naked, of course keeping a little privacy. Couldn't they advertise the soap without using a completely naked woman?

Some shows start morally clean then suddenly throw in a sexual scene. Before you can change the channel, if you do that, you have already seen too much. The scene has already registered in your mind waiting for an opportunity to be replayed. Truly, this matter of sexual intimacy is nothing new to anybody today. Many movies especially on Direct TV, Cable TV, Dish or any other network are filled with sexual scenes and some explicit ones too. Not only movies but also comedies are loaded with sexual overtones or talk. People are easily influenced by what they see. Choose wisely what you view on television or cable. The power button or channel button can be very useful when dirty movies are shown. If you don't have the authority to turn off the television, don't hesitate to leave the room. It's your mind and your life, and you have to guard it and keep it pure.

2. Videos, DVDs and Cell Phones

Videos, DVDs, cell phones and other electronic devices can also strongly influence the minds and behaviour of people. Through this electronic media, pornographic content is more explicit because they are unedited. The sex scenes are not cut or covered up in any way. Anyone has access to videos and DVDs, and some youths and singles look at 'X' rated movies in private and fill their minds with filth. People whose minds are filled with pornography (pictures, writings, etc. intended mainly to arouse sexual desire) end up doing things that they never thought they would do such as committing rape, incest or fornication. Sometimes parents leave their upstanding, respectable children at home for a few hours or an entire weekend unattended. Well, some young people embrace that as a golden opportunity to do everything their parents told them not to do. They go and rent some 'X' rated videos and DVDs. The parents return home unaware of what went on in their absence. A week later someone is raped in the community and the parents' son was held as the suspect. Immediately, the parents protest about how upright and respectable their son is. If they only knew the filth he was feeding his mind with in their absence, they would quietly say, "He is guilty."

Movies would be just as interesting without those sex scenes. Wouldn't they? There are many clean movies that you can look at without polluting your mind and weakening your defenses against sexual temptations.

3. Advertising

Advertising is one of the subtle strategies of the devil to present sex to people on a continuous basis. As mentioned earlier they appear on television even when the product advertised has nothing to do with sex. Billboards are also popular for showing almost naked people, even if a card is advertised. Some newspaper advertisements are also too suggestive and revealing for comfort. Beware of them.

22

4. Newspapers

You would expect to get news in the newspapers, but very often you get more than news: you get 'nudes.' In fact, the sale of some newspapers depends on the kind of pictures they publish. Less clothes mean more sales. Newspapers in that category seem to compete to see who could show the most nakedness without complete nudity. That is legal pornography. Christians who cherish purity should leave those newspapers alone because those images can linger in the mind and create problems now or later in life. You can get the same news from other newspapers.

5. Magazines

Some magazines can also entice people to sexual promiscuity. Pornography is the focus of such magazines. Newspapers are still a bit cautious, but magazines throw caution to the wind and show everything perverting the minds of young and old alike. Students sometimes carry such magazines to school and corrupt the minds of their peers. I hope you are not one of their victims because in the end it will be you to "ketch." If you have such magazines, you may be wondering what to do with them. The garbage bin or a grain of match could give you all the help you need.

6. Music

Music is also loaded with sexual lyrics. Too much music today is only "wine and jam," filled with seduction and promoting sexual promiscuity. Then the same people who sing, approve, sponsor, actively promote or listen to that type of music wonder why rape, incest and other forms of deviant sexual behaviour are on the increase. The slow intimate music or continuous pulsating rhythms accompanied by a few alcoholic beverages or other mind-altering drugs is a recipe for disaster in the form of lost virginity, unwanted pregnancies, fatherless children and spread of deadly venereal diseases including the killers, AIDS and HPV.

23

A wide variety of music today encourages sexual experiments. If the language is not plain, it is very suggestive of the sex act. Music videos and DVDs are also very aggressive in their promotion of the destructive message of free sex in their lyrics, antics and images that flash on the T.V. screen.

Young people really love music and often fall victim to this subtle trap of the devil when they fail to use discretion in their choice of music. It is unthinkable and unbelievable that youths who say they are Christians would buy or borrow CDs, cassettes, videos or DVDs with the destructive message of pre-marital free sex. A certain young Christian woman had no problems with a regular diet of ungodly music which eventually contributed to her backsliding. Beware of this music trap of the devil. Stay free from this trap so that you can really enjoy life and even help somebody else. Gospel music is the best choice for youths who wish to stay clean and committed to the Lord Jesus Christ. Gospel music provides an opportunity for worship, preserves purity of mind and promotes godly entertainment.

7. Internet

As useful as the internet is, it can also be very harmful. Both children and adults now have access to limitless information including pornography, unfortunately, with one click of the mouse. Sometimes a window pops up unexpectedly inviting you to or showing you a pornographic site. What should you do then? When that happens, don't hesitate to click the close or delete button immediately. That action should take care of that problem. Pay no mind to the heartless perverts who design such immoral sites. Save yourself.

Remember, not everything that is available on the net is good or should be explored. Don't pollute your mind with filth. If you take that bait, you <u>will</u> be caught by the evil

24

spirit of lust and immorality (sexual looseness). Be wise and leave those pornographic sites alone or block them if possible. Guard your mind.

8. Peer Conversations

Dirty talk cannot kill you, but it can influence you to make decisions and do things that will certainly kill you. Parents and guardians are often in the dark about what their children talk about or listen to when they meet their friends. They talk about everything from shoes to sex. I heard a form three student talking to another girl giving details of a sexual experience she had. Yes, in form three and sexually active. That was many years ago, and it's much worse now so much so that children in form two are eloping ('shacking up' or running away to live together).

In school, on the block, in the workplace and elsewhere, friends engage in dirty sex talk about what they have seen, heard, done or would like to do. When that happens in your presence, you have choices to make and action to take. For instance, should you stay and listen to their dirty talk? Should you add your little piece? Should you attempt to change the conversation? Should you try to ignore what is said or should you walk away when the conversation becomes dirty? What do you think is the best response? You are responsible for what goes into your mind and what goes on in your head. Remember, "garbage in, garbage out." Therefore, guard your mind, and keep your head clean because your life takes its cue from your mind.

With all these powerful negative influences surrounding you, it is very important for you to know what the Bible really teaches on sex and where to draw the line. I sometimes describe the devil as an octopus. His one aim is to destroy you, and he will use any means and anyone to do so. If you are in bondage or weak in any of the above areas, you should confess that weakness to God, and ask Him to strengthen you. Commit yourself to sexual purity at all cost regardless of the thoughts that fly through your head and the internal and external pressures that you feel, and you will certainly rejoice in time to come for making that stand. Make an effort to find out what the Bible teaches about relationships, sex and marriage, and strive to live by those principles, and you will most definitely live an overcoming life. The Bible says, *"Greater is he that is in you than he that is in the world"* **(I John 4:4b).** It means that if you have Jesus in your life, you have all the power you need to overcome temptations.

The Bible cautions us in **Matthew 5:27, 28** that *"... whosoever looks on a woman to lust after her has committed adultery with her already in his heart."* Women can also lust after men. Evil deeds start in the mind, so beware. Guard your mind!

It is said that the sexual urge is God-given and is a great blessing when enjoyed in the right context (that is, in marriage). It is also said that God has a high value of sexual relationships. In fact, sex is God's idea within the bounds of marriage. **Genesis 2:25** tells us that the man and his wife were naked and not ashamed. The first couple brought together by God enjoyed sexual relations only in marriage which is God's only plan for sexual activity. That's the way to go.

Be very careful with these

Chapter 5

FORNICATION

The question was asked, "Is anything wrong with kissing?" **Song of Solomon 1:2** says, *"Let him kiss me with the kisses of his mouth."* Someone might read that and say the Bible says that any woman can say to any man "Let him kiss me ..." or vice versa. The truth is that the two people mentioned in the verse are husband and wife, and the wife is inviting the husband to kiss her which is quite appropriate. It is inappropriate and wrong though for a single woman or man to ask a friend for a kiss or to ask to kiss that friend. I don't mean a kiss on the cheek on a birthday or other special occasion. I mean mouth to mouth. That is only for married couples in that verse.

Kissing "French style" often stirs up emotions that can tempt you to go further into fondling, necking and eventually the sex act itself. Then youths say I didn't mean to... Of course, you didn't mean to. Once you start getting physically involved and touching out of bounds areas, you naturally want to go further and further until you end up going 'all the way.' Then it is too late. You may ask how far can I go then? To even begin that journey is dangerous. You risk arriving at the point of no return. Remember, nothing can be done to undo the sex act. Fornication cannot be reversed. Once you begin the touching game, it is difficult to stop, and it is always hard not to go further the next time.

If you go down the road of kissing, you may end up at the destination of fornication. But what is fornication? **Fornication is having sex outside of marriage.** If you go down the road of necking and fondling, i.e. kissing the neck (leaving red marks on the neck as if "jep," jack Spaniard sting you) and touching private parts of another person's

27

body, you will end up in fornication thus losing your purity as an individual. If you don't want to end up at a certain destination, you better get off the road that leads there, and seductive touching is one of those roads.

If someone is willing to hide and have sex with you, chances are that they did or will do the same thing with someone else and you will never know. Of course, the person will lie and tell you that he/she never did it or will never do it with anyone else, and you are the only one for me followed by ah set ah sweet talk and 'mamaguy.' Lie! Doh fall for that.

Another danger is that people who commit fornication and didn't get caught tend to continue until they get caught. Getting caught doesn't always mean that people see them, but that it eventually catches up with them especially the girl who seems to be growing rapidly. Guess what. She is pregnant. Then the pressure starts. What to do now? What would my parent(s) say? What about school? What about church? How would I take care of the baby? Should I get married to the baby's father now? Or, should I just abort the baby and end everything?

To complicate matters, some people even get demon possessed when they commit fornication. Unlawful sex opens your life to demons that are just waiting for a chance to enter and live inside you. You may disagree and still want to take the risk. If it happens to you, then you will have no one to blame but yourself. Don't say, "That will never happen to me." **If you play with fire, you will get burned. Don't doubt that.**

Someone giving advice on AIDS prevention during the Carnival season (2002), said, "If you are in a tricky sexual position, try to get out without offending the other partner." Nonsense! Get out of it whether the person is offended or not. You have too much to lose and regret if you don't get out. If you have been travelling down the road of kissing, necking and fondling and find yourself in other sexually compromising positions, now is the best time to stop, get off that road and save yourself. It is better to be safe than sorry.

Biblical Truths about Fornication

Did you know the Bible says the following things about fornication? Check it out carefully and consider seriously as you read. In the Bible, fornication often includes all types of sexual sins including adultery. The verses mentioned below will show quite clearly what the Bible says about fornication. **I Corinthians 6:13** says, *"...Now the body is not for fornication but for the Lord; and the Lord for the body."* In other words, it is against the purpose of the human body to commit fornication. Put simply, the body was not made to fornicate.

The word fornication occurs twelve times in the book of Revelation. This shows that Satan will use fornication as a major weapon in the last days to destroy people, so beware. To be forewarned is to be forearmed. **Revelation 2:20** tells us that Jezebel will seduce God's servants to commit fornication. God's servants? Yes, God's servants. This surely reveals the strength of this temptation.

Why abstain from fornication?

Mark 7:21, 23 says, *"For from within, out of the heart of man, proceed evil thoughts, adulteries, fornications, murders ... All these evil things come from within and defile the man."* Two points from these verses are: (1) That fornication comes from inside the person and (2) It defiles or makes one dirty or unclean.

Revelation 2:21, 22 concerning Jezebel's sin described as fornication, God says, *"I have given her time to repent of her immorality/fornication, but she is unwilling"* (NIV). Verse 22 tells of her judgment for not repenting. **II Corinthians 12:21** indicates that there are people who do not repent of fornication. If you are guilty of fornication though, make sure you repent. God loves you, and He gives you time and opportunity to repent, but it would not be forever, so act now. How to repent is explained later.

Romans 1:29, 32 tells us that people who are filled with fornication are worthy of death or deserve to die. That is serious business. Also, **Colossians 3:5, 6** shows clearly that God will judge those who refuse to repent and stop the practice of fornication. **I Corinthians 10:8** gives an example of judgment when it says, *"Neither let us commit fornication as some of them (Israelites in the wilderness) committed, and fell in one day twenty-three thousand."* God is always right in His judgment, and He doesn't hesitate to judge when there is no repentance. **Jude 7** also tells us that Sodom and Gomorrah were judged because of fornication as an example for us to learn from.

Fornication is a serious sin that has serious consequences if there is no serious repentance. Of all the verses that warn against fornication, I think the sternest one is **I Corinthians 6:9** which states clearly that fornicators (those who refuse to repent of fornication) shall not inherit the kingdom of God. They will not go to heaven. If someone is not going to heaven, guess where he/she is going. You are right, straight to hell. That is very scary, but none of those judgments above have to happen to you. I don't want that for myself and I don't want that for you, so I plead with you to do the safe thing and stop fornicating and if you never did, don't ever start.

When you come face to face with the fierce temptation of fornication consider this your best and safest option.

Chapter 6

SEX AND MARRIAGE

Question: Sex only in marriage?

If God created us as sexual beings, why shouldn't I as a single person have sex whenever my body tingles? Why didn't you start eating solid meat when you were two months old? Because there is a time and place for everything. The Bible reveals that sex was created by God, but it was intended to be enjoyed at a certain time in one's life and only in the context of marriage i.e. only by legally married couples, not consenting adults. Therefore, any sex outside of marriage is an abuse of God's good gift and plan. **Genesis 2:24 and Matthew 19:5** tell us that husband and wife become "one flesh" through marriage especially through sexual intercourse. That "one flesh" expresses oneness and unity with each other. Therefore, a husband and wife become one through sexual intercourse.

There is a mysterious bonding that takes place when two people are sexually united. That bonding is often called "soul tie" which creates very serious problems for people who have sex before marriage. Sometimes people have sex before marriage and then want to get out of the relationship when they realize it will destroy them, but struggle to get out simply because of the soul tie developed with the sexual partner. They keep going back to each other when all the obvious signs tell them, "This will not work if we continue this relationship or even get married." Whether you remain unmarried, get married to each other or marry someone else, a soul tie creates serious problems.

This is so serious that the Bible says that if a man has sex with a prostitute, he becomes *one* with the prostitute

(I Corinthians 6:16). He becomes like the prostitute taking those ungodly qualities of loose living into his own life. Therefore, it's not just a little "fling." That has serious implications and consequences. Sex with anyone before marriage creates serious problems. You don't have to try it to find out. You can look around and learn from the mistakes of others. For instance, what would you do if you see someone jump off a 200-foot precipice and end up dead on the ground below? Would you try it to see if the same thing will happen to you? I think you would say no. It is a true statement that, "A wise man (person) learns from his mistakes, but a wiser man (person) learns from the mistakes of others." Look, listen, learn and live a pure, guilt-free and happy life.

Marriage or Common Law Living?

God's plan for two people who are interested in each other is to reserve sex only for when they are legally married. **Hebrews 13:4** says, "Marriage is honourable in all and the bed undefiled..." It is a honourable thing for two people of reasonable age who love each other to get married when other important factors are in place. When they get married, then they can engage in sex as often as they like, but never before. That verse also means that there is no room for common law relationships in God's plan. People who "shack up" (live common law) are blatantly disobeying God, and He will judge them. No two ways about that. An unmarried man and woman don't live together just for companionship. Get real. Common law living is not an option for the Christian or anybody who wants to please God and receive His blessings. That is pressure because there is no commitment by anybody, and anything could happen at any time.

Common law living is sin. People who shack up are living in sin. I speak to people in such a relationship from time to time, and they admit that they are living in sin. It is

33

fornication, which is any sex before or outside legal marriage. Governments may condone and sanction common law relationships, but God condemns it. Also, we have seen enough real-life examples of men who live in such relationships killing the lady then killing themselves. Status or rank does not prevent people who violate the principle of getting married from ending up dead. The highly educated and even lawmen get caught just like anybody else.

You may also be aware of examples where the woman got fed up with "licks" and pressure and killed the man. Stay out or get out of common law relationships and save yourself from all that trouble and God's sure judgment.

From my observation, most cases of murder-suicide are committed by people who live in common-law relationships. It horrifies me every time, but I wish people would learn from it. Young lady, play it safe, and don't sell yourself cheap by shacking up with any man. Young man, be a real macho man and *get married* to the woman you say you love. Do the dignified, righteous and honourable thing when the time comes and GET MARRIED. If you have been living with someone, now is a good time to make a commitment to each other to GET MARRIED soon. God **always** judges fornication and always blesses marriages. GET MARRIED and be blessed.

Whether you are involved in fornication or not, when you decide to get married, make sure you arrange to get counselling before you say "I do." Pre-marital counselling (counselling before marriage) is very, very important to a healthy marriage. Topics like love, communication, handling money, in-laws and of course sex should be discussed. This counselling should take place several months before you "tie the knot" even as much as six months before.

It makes a big difference to learn about marriage before you get married.

"It feels so good to be **married.**"

Chapter 7

HURTS OF UNLAWFUL SEX

Every time someone engages in ungodly and unlawful sex somebody gets hurt. It does not matter whether the offence is fornication, adultery, homosexuality, lesbianism or other sexual perversions, bad consequences follow. The following are some persons who get hurt and some of the consequences

1. Yourself

If no one else gets hurt, you are sure to get hurt when you have sex before marriage. In addition to a tormented conscience, severe guilt, careless lifestyle and reckless living, other things can go wrong.

(a) Pre-marital sex (sex before marriage) increases the chances of extra-marital sex/ adultery – having sex with someone else other than your marriage partner. That means if you were loose enough to have sex before marriage, when you marry it may be easy for you to have sex with someone else other than your marriage partner, and that is big trouble – too big to give details in this limited space. For instance, it could lead to a breakdown of your marriage, divorce, or even a murder suicide case.

(b) Pre-marital sex reduces the fulfillment of marital sex. If two people who are already involved in a sexual relationship do eventually marry each other, they often regret that they did not wait until their wedding day to enjoy the climax of mutual love. One couple said, "that one of their greatest regrets is not to have experienced that God-given blessing on their wedding night" because they had sex before they were married.

(c) You can get AIDS, HPV and other sexually transmitted diseases (STD's). Everyone knows that AIDS and now HPV are merciless killers, and they can be contracted from one sexual encounter. Some people have AIDS or other STD's and they don't even know it. They are not even sure who they got it from. Others have AIDS and they will not tell you because they are on a vengeance mission to spread the disease to you or any other reckless person. A girl got the HIV virus when she was eleven years old. As a result, she set out to infect as many men as she can before dying at age seventeen. She was successful. Some men got caught and they are now on the prowl spreading the disease themselves. The point is that the person you risk committing fornication with might just be someone with AIDS. To have sex with such a person is to sign your own death certificate just waiting to die.

You are probably still saying, "That will never happen to me." Hello! 'Wake up and smell the coffee.' The horrifying truth is that millions of people die of AIDS and HPV every year, and more than 40 million people worldwide have AIDS today. Most of them probably said, "That will never happen to me," but they were so wrong, and unless they get a miracle, they would also be dead wrong. Play it safe, abstain from unlawful sex, and don't become another AIDS statistic. If it happens to you though and you realize that you have the disease, don't spread it, but seek help immediately, and aim to make the rest of your life count for good.

(d) You can get pregnant if you are the female. If that happens, you have some serious decisions to make.

(1) Abortion.

That is murder. If you are already   guilty of fornication, don't add murder now to your list of offences. It will weigh very heavy on your conscience and body for a long time.

What if your mother had aborted you?

(2) Adoption.

That is giving up the child so that it will no longer belong to you but the family which agrees to take care of the child. You give up your right to own, nurture and bring up the child.

(3) Throw away the baby.

Only a heartless person with a deranged mind will do such a thing. This has happened too many times in our country already, and it is sad and outrageous.

(4) Have a 'shot gun' wedding.

People sometimes make quick plans to get married when they realize the woman or girl is pregnant. They think that getting married will solve their problems, but that isn't true. Very often they don't even know what the problem is, and they take that same problem into their marriage then later wonder what went wrong. They say, "We love each other" as if love is the only thing that makes a marriage last. Don't be deceived, a marriage needs much more than love to survive.

(5) Be a single parent.

Very often the man disappears after he gets you pregnant, and if he is around, he has no money to 'mind' a child. If he is around and has money, he may not be psychologically prepared for the responsibility of fatherhood. If you make up your mind to do the honourable thing and not commit murder by killing the child (abortion), you will have to 'mind' the child yourself because it was your choice to have sex with the man.

What would you do? Do you see that just having sex even one time before marriage creates all kinds of problems for you? I repeat, some people don't stop until they get caught whether by pregnancy, by someone who was there or passing by and they didn't know or by contracting some deadly disease. Others stop only when they end up dead. Sure, everybody will die, but why should you die like that before you really start to live? Don't insist on getting burned before you learn. Save yourself all that trouble, and leave sex until you are married to that special person God will send to you, and sex will be just as good then, even better.

2. Others

It takes two to have sex, and sex before marriage always affects the other person and sometimes even others. In fact, every time you have sex with someone you are not married to, you hurt that person. You thrust a dagger into the person's heart. That's the truth. Look at some of the ways you can hurt others.

(a) You steal someone else's virginity if it is the first time whether the person consented or not. Virginity cannot be replaced. You should have said NO! Virginity is one of the most valuable gifts that a single person has, and it should be preserved to be given after the wedding to the person one marries.

Until then, it is honourable and wonderful to be a pre-marital virgin (that is remaining a virgin while you are not married) among your peers who have given up their virginity in a 'cheap sale' or for free. It is no honour or achievement to give up your virginity for temporary pleasure or a few dollars when it is actually priceless and irreplaceable. It is more of a shame and dishonour to sell yourself cheaply. It doesn't matter whether it was pre-planned or happened suddenly under intense uncontrolled sexual pressure.

If you are a single adult, youth or high school student and still have your virginity intact, you should walk with your head up high that you are still pure and on the right track. If not, read on because help is on its way.

(b) If a sexual relationship does not last it could have a damaging effect on the person you might marry in future. If you are the female, you also have to beware of jealousy, resentment and possibly violence from the previous partner. If you are the male, you have to beware of the temptation to damage the woman who "dissed" you. It has happened before, so don't become another statistic.

(c) It could make marriage less likely by arguing that you already had sex   so what's the use getting married.

(c) It could make marriage less likely by arguing that you already had sex so what's the use getting married.

(d) You could contribute to the other person backsliding.

3. Society
Sex before marriage can lead to serious societal problems.
(a) <u>Family breakdown.</u>
It destroys the moral fabric of society. The number of struggling single parents and fatherless children can increase. Children born from such sexual relationships may be deprived of many privileges that other children have leading to severe psychological and other problems unless they are properly cared for and provided for.
(b) <u>Increasing crime.</u>
Sometimes children from such relationships rebel and get into trouble at home, school and later with the police because they lack the guidance they need to lead a respectable and constructive life. They may become a real menace to society unless they get saved.
(c) <u>Destruction.</u>
Increasing sexual promiscuity can invite the judgment of God upon the nation. The twin cities of Sodom and Gomorrah practiced sexual sins until they went beyond the point of no return. The deserved judgment of God fell and wiped those unrepentant, promiscuous cities off the face of the earth.

4. God
Sin always hurts the heart of God. It is impossible to love and serve God wholeheartedly and be disobedient in the area of sexual morality. In other words, it is impossible to live a sexually loose and scandalous life and receive God's favour and acceptance. God does not bless sexual immorality. He judges it. If you have hurt God by sexual immorality already, there is only one way out and that is through repentance. Repentance is saying to God, "I am guilty Lord and I am sorry. Please forgive me and help me never to do it

again." More details on repentance are given at the end of the book.

If you are a Christian whose greatest desire is to please God, then try to stay away from sex before marriage. Don't say you will use a condom. It is still sin, and many of the effects will still follow. Sometimes condoms are distributed freely to prevent the contraction of deadly diseases. However, there are two dangers associated with that diabolical practice. Firstly, it sends the wrong signal that it is alright to have sex before marriage once you don't get AIDS, HPV, get pregnant or get somebody pregnant. Secondly, it can lead some to experiment with sex and encourage others to continue to be sexually active. Watch out! Additionally, condoms are not 100 % safe. It's easy to fall into the sex trap and hard to come out of it, so the best thing is to stay out of it in the first place. Don't say that will never happen to me. It can and will if you take the risk. It doesn't make sense trying to prove something. Why not prove that you can live a pure and chaste life in a society that is obsessed with sex and being destroyed by it. Remember the only safe sex before marriage is "NO SEX." The only safe sex is "MARITAL SEX."

How does someone who is interested in you show love?

Is it by sex? No! Sexual intercourse is not the way to show love. In fact, anyone who wants to prove that he/she loves you by having sex with you doesn't love you at all.
Anyone who wants to have sex with you before marriage only wants to disrespect you and make a fool of you. If you want to have sex with someone before marriage, you are aiming to disrespect and make a fool of that person. That is not love but lust. Love gives, not takes. Lust takes, not gives. When you have sex before marriage, you take things from the person that you can never restore – their virginity and more.

The truth is that self-control shows more love and plenty

respect.

Another thing to bear in mind is that of influence. What kind of influence are you having on people around you and society at large? Influence is either positive or negative. Positive influences cause people to respect you and also create a better place for you and others to live. Negative influences cause people to disrespect you and also make the world a dangerous place to live. If you live by God's standard, in the long run, you will earn the respect of your peers. You will also have a positive influence on society and make the world a better place to live. It is my personal conviction that sexual promiscuity is the primary reason for the society being in the mess that it is in today. However, if you are a Christian, you will be able to influence others to serve Jesus when they see your words backed up by action. In other words, let us walk the talk by the way we live in public and in private.

I gone.

I didn't expect this, but it was my choice.

Chapter 8

SEXUAL TEMPTATIONS RECORDED IN THE BIBLE

The Bible records the sexual temptations faced by some people just like you and me without trying to cover up the reality of these pressures. The following examples of Bible characters who faced sexual temptations and how they responded can help us when we face similar temptations. Some of these examples may be familiar to you and some may not be. However, there is something important to learn from each example. Please study them carefully.

1. David and Bathsheba (II Samuel 11:1-5).

The account tells us that David stayed home during a time of war when he should have been in battle as the military leader. That evening he walked on the roof (houses were so designed) of his house. To his surprise, he saw a beautiful woman bathing. Ideas immediately came to his head. He probably stared rather than pulled away. His mind was probably racing 100 miles per hour. When he saw the presumably naked woman, he had choices to make – brush it off, turn away or make plans to sleep with her. Well, he chose the latter and sent for Bathsheba. She had no idea why she was called, but she responded promptly to the request and went to David because it was a privilege to be called by the king.

The Bible tells us that David had sex with her, and she became pregnant. Yuh think it easy. One time and he was caught. He tried a scheme to cover up his crime by engineering the death of the woman's husband, Uriah. With the husband dead and the child born, people probably assumed the child was Uriah's. David felt safe until the

43

prophet Nathan confronted him with his atrocious sin and said "You are the man" **(II Samuel 12:7).** Yes, David sinned, and it was exposed. He was caught.

The Bible says, "Be sure your sin will find you out" **(Numbers 32:23).** In other words, you cannot sin and hide it forever. If it is not genuinely repented of, it will be shamefully exposed at some time or another. Later David repented **(Psalms 51)**, and God forgave him, but he was judged. **II Samuel 12:10** says, *"Now therefore the sword will never depart from your house, because you despised me and took the wife of Uriah the Hittite to be your own."* Sin always has a price. However, we can learn from David by not repeating his mistake. Leave Bathsheba alone.

2. Samson and women (Judges 16:1-4).

Samson, the strongest man at the time, was chosen by God to lead Israel out of captivity which he accomplished for many years, but he had one major weakness which led to his downfall – love of women. **Judges 16:1** says that Samson went in unto (had sex with) a prostitute from Gaza. Talk about failure to control hormones. After that he fell in love with another woman named Delilah. It was that same woman, Delilah who seduced him and enticed him to reveal the secret of his supernatural strength.

That encounter with Delilah marked the beginning of the end of Samson's reign. Not surprisingly, he died shortly after. He could have accomplished much more, but he played with fire and he got burned. It happens every time. Sometimes women set fires (seduce) that destroy men, and men sometimes set fires that destroy women. Watch out for those "Delilahs" (men and women, boys and girls) who set traps to seduce and destroy you, and don't be a Delilah yourself destroying other people's lives. Rather stay pure and preserve your life.

3. Amnon and Tamar (II Samuel 13:1-15).

This is the shocking account of the outrageous act of a man named Amnon who was obsessed with his beautiful sister Tamar. He was frustrated to the point of being sick because he wanted to have sex with her but didn't know how to get her (verse 2). Together with his friend Jonadab, they came up with a scheme to get Tamar to his home. The account tells us that he eventually got her into his bedroom and raped her. A classic case of incest (forced sexual intercourse between two persons who are closely related). He knew it was wrong but he still did it because he lacked self-control badly. Incest is still wrong and very evil, and it leaves its victims crying in pain and some of them thinking about suicide years after the crime was committed. That pain can be healed by Jesus though.

The Bible tells us that after raping her, he hated her with a greater hatred than the love he had for her (verse 15). His hatred for her proves that he didn't love her at all but was only lusting after her. Anybody who tries to force or persuade you to have sex before marriage does not really love you but is only lusting after you hoping to get sex. A friend might say, "If you really love me..." Tell that person, "If you really love **me** you wouldn't ask me to do that." Real love is not shown by sex but by respect and consideration of the other person.

4. Israelites and Midianites (Numbers 25:1-9).

Israel was God's specially chosen people who were called to please Him in all things. Because of God's concern for His people, He gave specific instructions that they should not get involved with the women of the surrounding nations. Nevertheless, they disobeyed and slept with the women of Moab. This was so offensive to God that he commanded the execution of all those men. While others were weeping because of the judgment, one boldface man brought a Midianitish woman in front of Moses. Immediately, Phinehas got so mad with God's righteous anger that he took

45

a javelin and drove it through both of them killing them on the spot. The plague stopped immediately. That was a sin of sexual immorality and the unequal yoke, and it was judged severely.

That was a case of very harsh judgment. Twenty-four thousand people died in that judgment. God hates sexual sin greatly, and He will not compromise with anyone who commits it. If you indulge in sexual sin, you too will be judged. The good news though is that you can escape God's judgment by avoiding premarital sex and the unequal yoke.

5. Joseph and Potiphar's Wife (Genesis 39:7-16).

Joseph was a young godly Israelite who was sold into Egypt by his envious brothers. The Bible tells us that the Lord was with Joseph, and He made everything Joseph did to prosper. Potiphar observed Joseph's behaviour carefully then put Joseph in charge of his household. The presence of this young, handsome, prosperous man in the house got the attention of Potiphar's wife. She began to eye him. Not only that. One day she said to Joseph, "Come to bed with me," but Joseph refused by saying, "How could I do such a wicked thing and sin against God." Now, 'that is man.' She came to Joseph day after day, but he always refused to go to bed with her. Better yet, he even refused to spend time with her after that first day. That is really playing it safe. Again, 'that is man.'

One day when everybody was outside the house, she felt this was her best chance, so she grabbed him and said, "come to bed with me." She almost raped him. However, he didn't say, "what an opportunity." Instead, he left his cloak in the woman's hand and ran for his life. There was too much to lose for that one moment of pleasure. Joseph had his head on and did the right thing. He was later framed, accused of rape and then imprisoned for a crime he did not commit.

The story of his life teaches us that overcoming sexual temptation pays off in the long run. He became the president of Egypt directly under Pharoah and was used by God to bless many people. While God is trying to build character in us and make something beautiful of our lives, Satan is always trying to disgrace us and destroy us. Like Joseph, you can overcome sexual temptations, live in purity and make a positive contribution to society. You can be all that God wants you to be and do all that He wants you to do if you refuse to obey Satan and choose to obey God.

Chapter 9

BIBLICAL BASIS FOR OVERCOMING SEXUAL TEMPTATIONS

Once we live in this world, we will face all kinds of temptations including sexual temptations. Since that is so, does the Bible say anything about overcoming these numerous nagging, annoying and destructive temptations? Most certainly. The Bible gives clear guidelines on overcoming temptations and sexual temptations in particular. In fact, the Bible is the most reliable guide on how to live in victory in this world. Please pay close attention to the following verses and see for yourself.

James 4:7, 8a says, *"Submit yourselves, then, to God. Resist the devil, and he will flee from you. Come near to God and he will come near to you..."* (New International Version of the Bible, NIV). This tells us that overcoming sexual temptations or any other temptation begins by submitting and drawing near to God. Submission to God speaks of our willingness to **do whatever God says**. If you don't have a personal relationship with God, that submission begins by giving your life to the Lord Jesus Christ then obeying Him. Resisting the devil speaks of fighting against the devil and his suggestions. He tries to bring lustful thoughts to your mind to trap you. The more you give in to his thoughts, the more difficult it is to say no. The more you resist, the easier saying no becomes.

When facing a sexual temptation, you must ask yourself, what does God want me to do in this situation, and what is the devil trying to get me to do? What you do will determine whether God will be glorified and you get blessed or whether the devil will be glorified and you bring a curse and judgment upon yourself. Which do you prefer? The best thing is to submit to God and be blessed.

I Corinthians 6:18 warns, *"Flee fornication. Every sin that a man does is without the body: but he that commits fornication sin against his own body."* It is stated very clearly that our response to fornication is to flee i.e. to run for your life. No one sees a one-ton ferocious bull charging, and then goes up to the bull and politely asks to touch its nose. No way. You run for your life. You get speed that you didn't know you had. You can take on any Olympic gold medallist in that situation. That is how you should run from sexual temptation. The verse also tells us that fornication is a kind of sin that is different from all others. It is very deadly. Special judgment is pronounced on the sin of fornication. Avoid that judgment from coming upon your precious life by staying away from sexual sin. **The secret to overcoming is to flee.**

I Thessalonians 4:3, 4 says, *"It is God's will that you should be sanctified: that you should avoid sexual immorality (abstain from fornication); that each of you should learn to control his own body in a way that is holy and honourable."* (NIV). To abstain is 'to hold oneself back.' Sometimes a person is tempted to do something violent or otherwise wrong and cries out "Allyuh hold meh back." The Bible is saying that when you are tempted to fall into fornication, you have to hold your own self back. But you should not wait until you are in the presence of an inviting naked person to try to hold yourself back. It might be too late then. You have to learn to hold yourself back long before it reaches that far. **It will do you well to practice holding yourself back when the smaller temptations to kiss and fondle come.**

The verse also tells us that we should learn how to control

49

our bodies. Your body doesn't act on its own. You decide what it does, and you are responsible for whatever it does, so you can't say "The devil made me do it." Through the power of the Holy Spirit you can take control of your body so that you do what glorifies God. You can overcome sexual temptations. Yes, you can.

Chapter 10

WHAT IF I COMMIT A SEXUAL SIN?

You can overcome sexual temptation. Millions of people have overcome sexual temptations and continue to do so daily. People with Jesus in their hearts have all the power they need to overcome sexual temptations. If you have been overcoming sexual temptations, I encourage you to continue living the overcoming life and enjoy the benefits of purity. However, if you have slipped and committed a sexual sin, you may wonder if there is a way out. As stated earlier, some things about sex before marriage are irreversible, but there are some things that you can do to receive forgiveness and to face the future with hope, not repeating the acts of sexual immorality. Because of God's love for you, Jesus came into the world to die on the cross and shed his blood for all of your sins including sexual sins, so He made the way for you to be forgiven and free. If you really want to live in God's kingdom forever, you better get your life right with Him and live for Him NOW.

Whether you have committed a sexual sin or not, you need Jesus in your life because you have certainly committed other sins which separate you from God just the same. It takes only one sin to disqualify you from heaven. The fact is that every human being has sinned or done wrong things, and we all need the forgiveness of God if we want to live with Him forever. The way to get God's forgiveness and to be at peace with Him and yourself is to give your life to Jesus Christ and receive Him into your heart.

If you have never given your life to Jesus, that's the first step you must take to be empowered to overcome sexual and other temptations. I encourage you to take that step and experience God's power and victory in your own life today. This has been made possible through the death of Jesus Christ on the cross and His resurrection on the third day. In fact, you can take that step right now by praying the following prayer. **Mean every word from your heart as you pray.**

PRAYER: *O God, I am a victim of sin. I confess all my sins and the evil I have committed against you. I ask you to forgive me and cleanse me from all my sins by the blood of Jesus and save me. Jesus, I give my whole life to you now, and I ask you to come into my life and change me. Thank you God for saving me. Amen!*

Once you meant that prayer, Jesus has come into your heart and received your life. Now that you have given your life to Jesus, it is important for you to continue to submit to God and resist the devil to overcome temptation. However, if you sin, you should take the following steps.

As someone who has given your life to Jesus, you are moving towards perfection, and until that time you should take the following steps to deal with specific sins you may fall into. If you really want to be forgiven and free from the power of that sin, please take the following steps.

1. Go to the Father through Jesus Christ because He is your Advocate or the one who speaks to the Father on your behalf **(I John 2:1** – *"My dear children, I write this to you so that you will not sin. But if anybody does sin, we have one who speaks to the Father in our defence - Jesus Christ the righteous One"*). He is waiting for you to come to Him.

2. Sincerely admit and confess the sin by name to God with no desire to continue committing that sin, and God will forgive you **(I John 1:9** - *If we confess our sins, he is faithful and just and will forgive us our sins and purify us from all unrighteousness"* and **Proverbs 28:13)**.

3. Ask that the blood of Jesus Christ cleanse you from the specific sin by name (fornication etc.), and you will be cleansed **(I John 1:7b** - *"the blood of Jesus, his Son, purifies us from all sin").*

4. Forsake (give up) the sin **(Proverbs 28:13** - *He who covers his sins will not prosper, but whoever confesses and forsakes his sins will obtain mercy").*

Once you have repented sincerely, God has forgiven you. Now you can face the future knowing that your sins are forgiven and cleansed. They will not be held against you. Remember, you can overcome sexual temptation and have meaningful friendships that are nor based on sex.

Chapter 11

TEN WAYS TO OVERCOME SEXUAL TEMPTATIONS

1. Set boundaries for your life and live within them always.

Do a good survey of your own life and set clear, definite boundaries as your personal safety zone. When you set them, aim to live within them. You will understand however, that if you step outside the boundary, you will be putting yourself at great risk. There is more than enough room for freedom and fulfillment within the boundaries of sexual purity. Don't fool yourself by thinking that you can step over the boundary and still be safe. Never happen! The moment you cross that line you start to go down the drain of sexual immorality. Others have no boundaries. They get caught in the web of sexual promiscuity and see a spider called Satan staring at them as if he wants to eat them raw. Then they wonder how did I get into this mess? How do I get out? Don't fool yourself by thinking "That will never happen to me" if you step over the boundary line. Set boundaries of sexual purity and live within them and enjoy your life.

2. Keep your head on.

Both emotions and brains are supposed to function unanimously. However, when emotions respond to sexual stimulation, the brain gets serious trouble keeping up. It sometimes shuts down leaving the emotions free to run wild. ALWAYS THINK before you act.

3. Remember what fornication steals from you.

Remember that fornication steals more from you than it claims to give if it gives anything at all. In case you forgot, it steals your virginity, dignity, purity and other valuable assets.

4. Avoid secluded or dark places.

It is still true that prevention is better than cure. The secret to overcoming is sometimes as simple as refusing to go to certain places. Friends and lovers who frequent secluded and dark places and sometimes cars are setting themselves up for trouble. The intention might be to get some privacy, but instead that could be easily turned into irreversible sexual intimacy. It is simple, just don't go.

5. Avoid touching each other intimately.

Some people like to touch. Anything they see they want to touch, and if you wear clothing that allows your friend to see, that person might just want to touch. There is the casual harmless touch as well as a provocative sensual touch which should be avoided. As far as the human body is concerned, certain areas are out of bounds for unmarried people. Consequently, you should be diligent to keep your hands in check and remove your friend's hands when they are trespassing.

6. Say "NO!" and mean "NOOOO!"

Love and sex are not the same. Your friend might drop a line giving you the impression that the best way to prove your love is by sex. How would you respond? A good way to save yourself in this situation is to simply say "NO!" and mean "NOOOO!" This "NO!" is not a whisper with a smile on your face or a "NO" accompanied by "Well..." Don't say "NO" as if you are thinking about your friend's suggestion. Your "NO" must be a strong bellowing "NO!" that's loud enough and louder than conversational volume if necessary, to send a clear message that you mean "NOOOO!" and no joke about it. Repeat "NO!" and even ask "which part of the word 'NO' don't you understand?" if your friend persists.

7. Leave the scene immediately.

Some people give in to temptation simply because they remain in the environment of temptation too long. They linger, observe, think and wonder what to do. At the first sign of danger and arousal, you should run for your life. Don't even wait to apologize for your sudden departure. Just leave. Remember, an ounce of prevention is better than a pound of cure.

8. Call on Jesus for help immediately.

Some people are afraid to say "I need help." However, when it comes to sexual temptations, don't hesitate to call on Jesus for help. Call on Jesus immediately. He is always there willing and able to help you. Ask the Lord to cover your mind with the blood of Jesus.

9. Remember the warnings of God.

Temptation is not sin, but giving in to the temptation is sin, and sin always has bad consequences. Therefore, remember God's warnings against sin because God's Word explains clearly that He judges sin. You can overcome temptation and escape judgment.

10. Make a covenant with God.

Make a covenant with God to remain a virgin until marriage and keep a symbol like a ring or chain as a constant reminder. This covenant could take the form of a pledge or prayer of commitment to chastity and abstinence. To reinforce your covenant, you can tell a friend of the same sex and be accountable to that person.

Now that you know these practical principles for overcoming sexual temptations, the responsibility is yours to live by them and you will never become a victim of the sexual predators out there. I sincerely urge you to live your life with the firm commitment to apply these principles. Then you would be able to say with unshakable confidence, "That will never happen to me."

FINALLY

Thank you for taking the time to read this book. I hope that it has encouraged you in some way in your life's journey. I wrote this book specifically to help youths and singles to live a chaste and godly life that will please and glorigy God. The contents of this book is also useful to parents and people who work with youths. Also, if you read this book and you never received Jesus Christ into your life, you can go back to the prayer on page 54 and pray it to do so.

Now, as you close this book, I want to kindly ask if you can write a short review for me please on my Amazon.com book page if you purchased it there or if not, send to me at **gplace500@gmail.com** while the content is still fresh in your mind.

If you like this book and would like to see or read parts of some of my other books, then go to the Amazon.com page and type books by Richardson George in the search bar. Click on the cover of any of my books. Then click "Read sample" under the next cover that comes up and begin reading. Enjoy!

Thank you and God bless you.

Sincerely,
Richardson George

OTHER BOOKS BY RICHARDSON GEORGE
(Available on Amazon also)

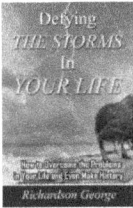

DEFYING THE STORMS IN YOUR LIFE
This book explains how to overcome the unavoidable storms we face in life to which many unfortunately succumb. The entire book is based on the incident when

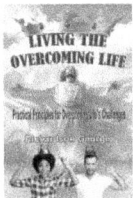

LIVIGN THE OVERCOMING LIFE
This book gives practical principles and strategies for overcoming life's challenges such as rejection, misunderstanding, unforgiveness, negativism, impatience, revenge to mention a few and is based entirely on the life of Jesus Christ.

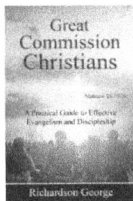

GREAT COMMISSION CHRISTIANS
This book gives several practical strategies for personal and church evangelism. It spells out exactly how to do one-on-one discipleship with new believers and gives a strategy for church planting.

FORGIVE
This book explains biblical forgiveness and outlines a very practical and easy to implement step by step process to forgiving others.

USE WHAT YOU HAVE

This book, based on the healing of blind Bartimaeus, addresses negative mindsets that keep people, even multi-millionaires stuck on undesirable pavements like depression, addiction etc. on which many die. God created you with a purpose and gives you everything you need to fulfill that purpose.

INTERVENTION

This is a practical, inspirational, biblical book on restoration which strongly encourages the reader and motivates him/her to restore others who may have fallen.

DESARROLLANDO DISCÍPULOS DINÁMICOS

This book is the Spanish translation of my English book Developing Dynamic Disciples.

THAT WILL NEVER HAPPEN TO ME

A small book for youths and singles dealing with the big issues of love, relationships and abstinence. Read 10 practical ways to overcome sexual temptations.

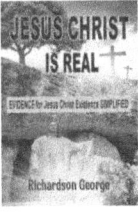

JESUS CHRIST IS REAL

This book gives convincing simplified evidence for Jesus Christ as a real historical character in a unique way. Apologetic in nature.